THE DEPTHS OF ANIMA

POEMS BY

KAI ADIA

Copyright © 2020 by Kai Adia

Published by Bee Infinite Publishing

All rights reserved.
No part of this book may be reproduced or used in any manner without permission of the copyright owner except for the use of quotations in a book review. For more information, address: kai@kaiadia.com

www.kaiadia.com
www.beeinfinite.org

Published in Los Angeles, CA

FIRST EDITION

ISBN 978-1-7360038-0-0

Cover design: Kai Adia

CONTENTS

Introduction	4
Anima	5
Cenote	6
Seeing	9
Bodied	10
Spaceship	11
Mariposas	12
Fear Less	14
Dive	16
Wanting	17
Their Tears	18
Walking To Hummingbirds	20
Koi	23
Pyrophytic	24
Who's Looking?	25
Dying Stars	28
Strange Animals	29
Great Brown Bird	31
Floating	32
Akasha	34
Safety Drills, Karmic Bonds	35
Brown Girl	36
Prayer	37
Gestating	38
Wake Up	39
Hope Is Esperanza	41
Birth	42
Splat	43
The Misuse of Forgiveness	45
Afrofuture	47
Clearing	48
Adsum	50
The String	52
Notes	53
Acknowledgements	54

INTRODUCTION

When I write poetry, it is a direct line to how I feel or what I experience. I noticed this when I would jot down notes in my journal or on my phone. *The Depths of Anima* is thus a culmination of stories and recollections that I have written over the years in poetic form. These poems have helped me to navigate how I feel about anxiety, overthinking, as well as my thoughts on spirituality and the environment that carries us all. This poetry collection is about noticing the outside world and the one inside too.

In the Carl Jungian sense, Anima is the feminine unconscious of the male psyche. *The Depths of Anima* challenges this school of thought by introducing an interpretation of Anima as the feminine spirit living in all of us. She's the inner voice, the soul, urging us to see ourselves fully when we might lose sight of our truest nature. The poems I share mark the journey to pull Anima out of our unconscious minds so that we can speak to her, listen to her, and, finally, embody her.

I want to share 'Anima' with you so you can take time to make meaning of what you experience. So often we are caught in the commotion of our lives that we don't even realize we have tunnel vision, thinking the way we live is the only way. It is my sincere hope that once you read each poem you will be moved to slow down, just a little, and be sentient with the world around you.

In addition, I acknowledge *The Depths of Anima* is written on indigenous land. I'm grateful to the Tongva people and other indigenous communities who continue to steward this space and place.

ANIMA

Soul hovering
Free of time
She's always talking.
Sometimes she's quiet
like a bustling bee
nuzzling close to your inner ear
Like a flower,
or she's loud like the drone of an airplane
Cutting through the air,
shaking your entire consciousness.

Let her speak.

CENOTE

Get quiet until you are empty.
I heard emptiness is a blessing.
Emptiness, like stillness, makes everything slow down.
It is hard to be empty when the radio mind is always talking.
In this space ideas, thoughts, and that particular action
become abstracted, magnified, stretched, and pulled apart
until it's unrecognizable.

I'm not always sure what writing is to me.
Am I infatuated with words?

When I close my eyes, I am a cenote.
Somewhere light peaks in from the collapsed bedrock of me,
illuminating the subtle water underneath. It is a constant stream.
Words are the droplets that clump together
and become more than what they are alone.
Water that is ancient and dormant.
Water that merges with the newest of itself that falls from the sky.
And the rains were sparse that year.

I remember I had a binder filled with loose-leaf pages.
The story written never seemed to end.
It was about nothing and I didn't care.
There were no restrictions, it was just me and Story.

As I write, my eyes become misty.
Something inside of me is saying I missed you.
I missed when our fingers tapped and made letters.
Letters as deep as static noise.
Letters solid as droplets pulled into ice.

As something inside of me urges to cry
formulating tears to run from my eyes,
it is a feeling rather than a thought.

It is something that's always been.
It is something that cannot be rational.
It is something that can be hurt.
It is something that will be healed.

SEEING

A tidepool is a window.
There are flowers in the ocean.
Stuck to the tan rocks is
the squishy brown flesh of an anemone.
I stroke the side of its plush-soft body.
Upon my touch, the anemone releases
translucent blue-green tentacles.
They fan out like flower petals.
The flower of the ocean.

The petals latch onto my finger
sending a peculiar sensation of mild shocks. Defense.
(It just felt sticky and ticklish to me.)

Maybe the tentacles are the eyes of the anemone,
and it's getting an image of me.
I'm probably a strange creature
possessing no face, fins, or even tentacles like it.
I suddenly want to be small,
like one of the gray fish darting about,
and be in this world.
If I were smaller, the anemone could look at all of me
then we could really see one another.

BODIED

in Earth school
we go straight to the head
nobody teaches anybody
how to live
in a body.

get comfortable with your form, they could say.
(i guess we learn it all along the way.)

if we must learn anything
in Earth School
it's to stop telling other people
how to
feel
grieve
express their joy
sit in their silence.

just show me how to love my body.

SPACESHIP

It's just a scratch on the spaceship
The crew is unshaken, able
To steer the inky black.

The cool metal shivers like skin
When dirty debris grazes its fingers against you
Taunting insecurities to rear from the cage
You locked and threw away
It dangles behind
Tethered, out of sight

Only a scratch!
You think the fingers have slashed into your core
Hacking into your mainframe
Coding in shrieking whispers:
you're not enough
you won't survive

The skin ripples at the contact
You want to rip across the eons
Until you're where you need to be
Flag staked, settlement planted, society thriving

Remember
The light from distant fireballs
Travels unafraid
of being consumed by the vastness
To meet your eyes.

MARIPOSAS

Butterflies and moths are the same.
They are both mariposas
in Costa Rica.
When a great brown moth flies
into the room,
Mi Mama Tica laughs.
I have shrunken into my shirt.
I must articulate why I am frightened.
I do not have the words to explain
in this different tongue.
She can *shoo* them away or
pick them up by their wings
toss them outside,
out of confinement.
Moths have bigger bodies,
bigger eyes to see
the dark.
Their papery wings flutter so minutely
Gasping
        Reaching
                Straining
                        To fly higher.

FEAR LESS

How can I fear
less?

Maybe I must write fear
to let it go.
I'll look at it
I'll feel it
I'll cry from it
I'll heal from it.

Putting an old self on the page,
I see her inadequate fear,
forgive her,
let her have her time,
and let her be relieved.

I suppose I fear what my body tells me
when my chest feels clouded
when it seems I can't relieve it,
when I don't know where the tears come from
or why they fall.

I put an old self on the page.
Like a dragonfly stalled in the wind,
the papery wings aren't as delicate as they seem.
It is something that will be healed.

Feeling an inkling of the deepest cutting doubt
I imagine hands upon my head,
shoulders, back, legs, and feet.
They hold me, Black and Brown palms.
Their hands tell me
I am supported, protected, never alone
Always loved

Are they the hands of the Past and Future
Together
In unseen spaces?

I think someone told me eons ago
To hold onto my words
Keep everything in
Maybe it's the experiences gathered
Lashes on my skin
Tearing my psyche
Saying: keep what you can close to chest
Hold it in so deep
underneath
the barrier of broken skin.

I say: let it out, now.

DIVE

I want to dive into the ocean
without the encumbrance of needing
to come up for air.
Maybe then I will not fear my weightlessness
Or the black depth at the bottom.
I will twist and twirl
Knowing I'm awash in a tidal wave
of Joy.
It crashes through me
At once I tumble,
shaken.
Rolling in the rush
holding my breath,
seizing myself
until I realize
I can breathe here too.

WANTING

sometimes I want land.
maybe those forty acres
to make something for us

a space

a place

we don't need them.

the birds and other beings
would follow us
out of cages
out of fakeness
and they could have themselves.

THEIR TEARS

Maybe the tears aren't my own.
They are the salty streams
Of those who hoped for better,
Who had the audacity to know
Inside themselves that they were enough.
Others spat in their faces
But they held that feeling steadfast
In their chests
Applying the pressure
Of rebellion
Stubbornness
And hard love
Until a precious
Piece of their
Brilliance
Coagulated.
And now, they cry
Inside of me
Seeing that I would let
Their jewels
Fall

Even when the jewels feel heavy
Enough to be simple jagged stones
Or ordinary enough to be put down,
I must remember their nature
No one can recreate them.
It would only be a poor imitation
It is through me their jewels
Be appraised for what they are worth
Priceless gifts
Given with the hope of
Careful   Tender   Remembrance

I'll make sure they are remembered, cherished even
So the tears they cry
Turn to those of irrevocable
Happiness.

WALKING TO HUMMINGBIRDS

I have touched two hummingbirds
One was Alive
One was Dead
Both times I was alone, walking
When they were on my path.

I thought Alive was hurt.
It sat in the middle of the narrow pavement.
I remember that day I was confidently alone
Tucked away in my thoughts.
I saw a movie and even
Ate a sweet slice of pie.
It was drizzling, I remember
because I had my umbrella.
I walked back to campus
there it was on a path I usually don't walk
because it is so small and awkward to navigate
when someone on a bike is close ahead
or right behind me.
But the path was clear
Seeing Alive, I dropped down
to get it out of the way.
I didn't want some careless person to crush it.
I scooped it up, it let me.
I placed it on a rock, it tumbled.
I tried to place it on a flat surface again,
hoping I didn't hurt its injured wing.
After my second attempt, it SPRANG up!
UP into a small tree
A flurry of green wings, it flew.

I thought it was hurt
It was resting.
It was waiting.

When I saw Dead
I wondered if it was balled-up paper, at first.
Looking closer,
I gasped, springing out of my thoughts.
It was so still, so small.
A colorful lump on pavement.
I wanted to get it out of the way
so no one would smash its body.
I got a stick and pushed it,
it rolled.
I thought that was crude
so I picked it up.
Its feathers were so soft, so small.
I put it on the dirt
at least it was close to something
it knew far better than me.
I wanted to do more for Dead
I wanted to dig a hole for Dead
Say a prayer for Dead
Something about Dead
made me pause
made me feel
made me see.

What had burned it out
so that it fell from the sky
to land on pavement and die
next to a door where humans walk by
so in their own worlds
They wouldn't even see you
Dying
Even if there was still time to save you?

But Dead, I saw you.
I stopped for you.
I felt you.

KOI

Did they know they were on display for human eyes
to watch and dismiss?
They swam with their naked spotted bodies,
gulping the murky black water.
The koi had such simple lives: going around in circles
floating and drifting about with the same fish faces.
I wonder if they ever get bored or hide things from one another.
Then their lives wouldn't be so different from ours.
We circle around locations that define our lives too, don't we?
Work. School. Home. Bed. That cafe.
Even our thoughts are recycled in our minds
then regurgitated onto this world.
At least the koi have the bliss of unthinking.

PYROPHYTIC

you don't know who you are
until the heat turns on.
when you are scorched by fire
withstand the heat
observe
wait for it
to bathe you.
(i've chanted in the fire)
you can either turn to ash
consumed by the friction of fear
or open from your sleep by the swoon of smoke.
(no matter what, the fire will uncover your true form)
the rising wisps can spell
a possible future.
(i prayed to see light)

a world's chaos can feel like
a passage of fire.
you might be the seed that needs it
to melt your resin
of passivity and comfort.

WHO'S LOOKING?

I like to be alone
More often than not
I am my best companion
One day I left a cafe
Traversing the inner city roads
bypassing makeshift beds and singular people
I strolled the wide main streets
Seeking sweet açaí.
When I went home
My mom asked me where I'd been
How I'd spent my day
I told her
Almost proud
And she looked at me
Disbelieving
I would walk such blocks.
She wanted me to tell her I was
Kidding
Lying
But I wasn't.
If she believed in hitting
I'm sure she would have slapped me
Instead,
She scolded my naïveté.

I always thought
(Maybe it's been hardwired)
That fabled deviants
looked at petite girls with blond hair
And I was protected by seeming
Unseeable
Undesirable
I didn't understand the duality
Imposed
on girls like me

Assumed valuable and valueless.
But, mom assured me that the issue
wasn't simply being snatched
It was that no one looked for Black girls.
No one sent search parties in our honor
To rescue us like princesses.
If they did
200 of us wouldn't have gone missing.
Girls like me
wouldn't be ignored
when they don't show up
for school after months of absence.

So always tell her where I am.
If someone hopes to trade my body
I may have a chance of being found.
No matter popular bias,
She and Father would never
Let me be forgotten.

I don't believe it has to be this way
Nor does she
Because we see
Girls like us
We stand for
Girls like us.

Maybe we're all fed lies.
Thick lies that stay in our throats.
But, if you'll uncling your fingers
From the homey bowl of stew
I'll help you unlearn the lie
Of some knight
Either ironclad or wielding a gun and fighting fists
Coming to rescue
The Girls.

Close your mouth
And know
One way or another
Girls turn into Women
Who show up
And try to save
The Girls.

DYING STARS

Where are the starfish?
Aren't there supposed to be starfish?
The guides for this trip told us that they were dying.
Something in the water
was causing the stars to secrete white puss
and waste away.
He even showed one to us, dead on the gray sharp rocks.
It looked like mucus or bird poop.
On another rock, I swore I saw a splat of white mucus
that was once a starfish.
Did it inhale the crashing waves
that showered its home daily
and taste a difference?
Did the poison sneakily settle in the star
when it projected its stomach out of its body to feed?
I stared at the spot and then looked away.
My classmates saddened for a time
Went back to walking on the rocks
with their bare feet and laughing.
How could I marvel at the clear water,
observe the tiny life,
and not see the starfish?

STRANGE ANIMALS

People are strange animals.
We've placed value in something
that cannot breathe life
doesn't grow from the sun's blaze
yet we believe it gives us life
Though we most assuredly know it doesn't grow on trees.

Our fascination with it manifests into consumer things.
Flamboyant distractions too.
It's led us to see the diversity of nature
as "ecosystem services"
only existing to fulfill our wants.
No, the false green was constructed,
like many social systems,
by strange animals
and put in place to divide us
from what really and truly is.

What is, is the Earth.
What is, is the rainfall that infiltrates soil
is stored as groundwater, once safe
enough to drink.
What is, is balanced greenhouse gases help sustain warmth
so that Earth can have
forests, oceans, glaciers, predators, prey, and microbes that eat decay.
And us, strange animals.

There is a flow to which we are out of touch.
(Some more than others. Some don't need
to be reminded of intrinsic value.)
But, strange animals pump, frack, and burn
the liquid essence of long-dead organisms
and wonder why ultra-fine particles dance in our lungs
and project a photochemical haze blocking blue sky.

We produce and consume,
We produce and consume,
We produce waste and consume too much.
It's time to remember
The only balance in nature
is Change.
Nothing is stagnant.
Nothing is pristine.
Forget constructs
and adapt to flow.

The Terrarium is well made.
What is, doesn't have to be what was.

GREAT BROWN BIRD

Soar high, swoop low.

I had my dinner boxed
and warm in my hands.
I was talking to someone I haven't seen
or spoken to in a while.
We ran down the semester,
how we kept to ourselves.
In this atmosphere
If you aren't doing things with people,
eating every meal with people,
you are strange
and missing out.

We crossed the street; at once
a great brown bird
swooped into our vision
Flying low then taking off
to sit on a lamp post.

My acquaintance was scared
thinking of how those great birds can pick up babies.
Transfixed, I kept staring.
She wanted to get far away,
I wanted to get closer.

We split, saying our goodbyes.
I walked to the lamp post.
The hawk rose again,
holding something in its talons
it swooped right above my head.
To a tree where it could be concealed
and eat its dinner in peace.

FLOATING

Sitting on a small bridge,
koi fish swam under me.
I wanted to dip my feet or even my hands in
and touch one of them. Or all of them.
Large ones and small ones,
varying in color but moving like one body.
I closed my eyes.

Slowly, I laid on the darkness.

The water held me effortlessly in its cool grasp.

Softly, it lapped around all of my edges

loosened my hair from the braids that bound them.

The koi joined in,

with their little mouths they unraveled the thick strands.

Freely, the cool water rushed in, caressing

my scalp and soothing my tightly wrinkled brain.

The koi went to work too.

Some inched closer, pressed their lips and pulled.

They drew out inky thoughts

dispelling them to the water's depth.

Others swam around my body, forming one multicolored body.

They circled, around and around.

Heat radiated from them, reaching into my skin.

They swam and dispelled; it was tireless work.

AKASHA

Down the white sand steps
I approach the ocean.
At times I sit at the wandering edge.
I let it draw in and out,
clumping sand to the underside
of my legs.
This time, I step in.
I walk until I must swim.
With every stroke of my arms,
I am drawn
Closer to a dark blue creature.
She swims and sings
next to me.
Her great eye watches me
Until I am ready
To sing her song.

SAFETY DRILLS, KARMIC BONDS

In times of panic
I see we're just coasting.
It feels like we hitched a ride
To get to this plane
(We had to come through some way.)

Subjected to trauma,
We're left to our own devices.
(Do we actually care about each other?)
When we share our fear
It's like you see hysteria
Or maybe it's a truth
You are hardly equipped to face.
Again, The Girls have to save themselves
(It must be time for us to move on.)

Filled to my limit
I sometimes want to unzip this skin
(Find out what it's all really for)
Pull-on the string until I'm yanked back to the beginning.
I'll hear the Sound that started it all.

Are we the jumping microbes of some great walking beast?
Are our injuries and loneliness
Just the motion of us rubbing together
On the hide of this ceaseless, moving creature?

BROWN GIRL

Brown girl reaches her hands to the sky

  A great brown bird
  Quickly reaches down.
      The fatal talons encircle her wrists
      Her fingers wrap around the feathered legs.

     | Brown girl is plucked from the concrete.

    To her dazzled eyes
    Wings seem to block the whole sky.
    They raise her into the wind
    As if she weighs nothing.

Her dress flourishes around her thighs
Shimmying like feathers.

PRAYER

Magick is prayer.

Send your desire out of you

with focalized intention.

Will yourself to trust

that something good

on the Otherside

heard your call

heard your honeyed Heart

And is working . . .

GESTATING

I pray
Like anything it is a seed
That needs time
to grow.
As I shift states
Anxious
to Faithful
I call to Source
(pure connection)
To know it as my life
To remember
I am never separated.
Everything I seek
is revealing itself
As me.

WAKE UP

When's the wake up call?
Will it be a gunshot
And the sound of the next body's fall?
Pale hands on black keys pushing
Down
Down
Down
Until they bend and makes sounds
Their ears love to hear
Whether it's Black voices running melodic hymns
Or wheezing a haunting note

We wheeze until spores pour from our throats.

When's the wake up call?
The chemicals in our bodies are jostled
By supremacy displays
These constant sacrifices
Call for constant debate
We get the shakes and tremors
Afraid to make a misstep, take on a mistake
Shall we feel the knives and needles
Or numb ourselves with our favorite vice
Binge watching reruns at night
Just to breathe again.

When's the wake up call?

Will it be a gunshot

And the sound of the next body's fall?
(Must we stay here and face it all?)

In the middle of stillness
Someone is still killing us
Mask on. Silence gone.
Don't Stop. Don't Halt.
The pavement knows our soles.
Orange butterfly wings float with us
Tenderly sharing the Otherside's love.
Keep on with your warbling note
Chanting into the megaphone
Talk over the talking heads,
Open mouths gaping like mad fish
Saying anything to re-engineer
The narrative to be remembered
Casting a mirage
That "improper" behavior warrants
Our execution
When we're just
Jogging, playing, relaxing in our own homes.

The deep brown woman with the black puffy hair
Her fist in the air
Her voice echoes into the ether
Sending out freedom vibrations
Slipping between atoms
Holding our wishes, moving
Ahead of us
To open a
Future

HOPE IS ESPERANZA

When a green hopper is on your window
Don't walk there to pluck your index finger against the glass
Hoping your menacing reverberations will scare it away.
No, look with your open eyes
Find its green ones.
If it stays,
It is speaking.

> When I left my light on
> In Mi Mama Tica's house
> You hopped out of the night
> A flash of green
> You went to the brightest
> Point of light
> Streaking across my vision in the process.
> My instinct was to shriek
> Mi Mama Tica
> Came running to me
> With her, panic turned to laughter
> She called you Esperanza.

Hope is on your window
Staring at you
Speaking with it's waving antennae
Listen to its calm
And know it as your own.

BIRTH

The hospital had a roundabout
walking path on the fourth floor.
we went outside to walk with
the swollen bellied woman.
Encircled, we walked
timing the distance between contractions
Soon it would be time to welcome Luna.
As we made our way around
a red speck gently floated by us.
It leapt from the splayed hand of a tree
where many more of its kind settled.

The sweet beetle flew around us,

showering its affinity

for prosperity,

safe arrivals,

new beginnings.

SPLAT

In no way am I perfect.
I don't even pray
For perfection.
I ask that the next time
I feel lower than the soil
I turn to something
Higher
I wrench myself
Out of mind
To fall into something
Benevolent,
Sweet.
A Truth
Declaring
Healing in progress
Moving the body helps.
Doing a round of forward bends
Splayed hands and flexed feet,
I turn myself into geometry.
Like love, I return
to every fragmented
Piece
Scattered when I came
Splat
Onto this plane.

THE MISUSE OF FORGIVENESS

The body is Sacred.
The body is Spiritual.
And Our mortal bodies are disrespected.
Yet we are asked to do labor
Heave up our trauma onto our backs
So they can't see it
So we can't see it
So we forget it but still feel it
Weighing on our backs.

They say,
Release yourself from pain
Put it behind you.
While you're at it,
Expect no return of goodwill
But always be of goodwill.
Everything will be okay, they say
Submit and obey
And everything will be okay.
Now, articulate yourself
Without the friction of
Real emotion.

I ask,
What is absolution
if someone hasn't even realized they're wrong?
When they can't see person to person,
Only person to object,

Why absolve them?
I know forgiveness to be personal.
When it's put on screen, announced
We force healing and we don't see change.

The same people are constantly twisted.
The same people
Screaming for time to heal their bodies
The same people
Searching for resources to mend the inner sanctum
Are expected to submit and cure the ills of society in quiet corners.

I say,
Tell me why Black and Brown people suffer?
It can't be for a lack of forgiveness.
So Tell Me.

Maybe those who inflict hurt
Need to do their inner work
And ask to be forgiven.
Don't expect it with entitlement.

Better yet,
Bypass me and my kin completely
And ask Your God for forgiveness
Since He might be more benevolent than me.

AFROFUTURE

Today is now tomorrow
the shift happens in darkness,
worlds are created in darkness,
inside of me is darkness.
Look down my throat,
you will see
the space that lives between stars
a darkness
no word can fathom
it teems with power
to create...

This power is instilled in our bodies.
Darkness in various shades.
Darkness cultivated from this earth.
We flourish
populating this earth
with our brilliance.
People have the nerve to forget
what we started,
but we know
there is nothing without darkness

no language

no culture

no science

no power

We reflect the cosmos.
Today is now tomorrow
we must revel
in our darkness.

CLEARING

As I circle,
Wondering how to get out,
I've been building
Knowing
Every time my foot rises
It will fall on solid ground
Just keep going
One more step
I grow every millisecond

The clear voice of Anima
The pitter-patter of her biorhythm
Dissipates the mist
I step where it's thinner
Coming right to the surface
Emerging from the fog
I see I've been hiding
In the low swells of her voice
The raspy reserve, strained
from her never-ending
Encouragements

I grow every millisecond
Touching the dermal layer of my skin.
She speaks the story of
My essence sinking right in
Reaching out,
Touching you.

ADSUM

Say this word
and you are free
Adsum, I am here.

My life and my words
are sewn together
to craft my 'I am.'
It is rooted in a good foundation,
swaying with soulful beats
and deep hearty moans.
No longer is my voice not valid.

Skin soaked in sun rays
hair dense and rich as forests.
In me is the source of my love
Indeed.
Not a seeker.

Who can make a page have a voice,
to melt the ears of others,
but those who've reached inside themselves
to find what strums inside of them.

In the witching hour, my mind unlocks.
I bob my head to a sound only I can hear
thoughts slow then
to meditate on the 'I am.'
The audience under the wrinkled mind is hushed.
I submit to the magnificence of the sistah.
A finder.

Mystical pool of water,
light shines into me
illuminating the rich blue of me,

through the many depths
and droplets of water that connect.
Here, I am
Whole

In the lightness
and the darkness.
In both directions
Complete

Adsum,
I a m f r e e

THE STRING

I hope on the Otherside
We're shown the string
The one with every moment of our lives.
The conductors will let us touch them
Most of all, we'll watch
As it's put in rotation
Joined with other strings
And played
As another point of light
Dispersing its image, a pixel
Telling its independent story
That somehow connects
To the next one
And the next one
We'll be gobsmacked
By how it all fits
Yet the flickery bits
The ones out of focus
Will catch our attention
Remarking the times of our confusion
Disillusion
Pain received and inflicted
We'll see how it all could have been
Different
        Shortened
                Bypassed completely
Choices made and choices felt
Some of us will cry in shame over what we did
Lamenting how if only we could have remembered . . .
But the conductors will gently share
How the scale of time and experience converge
On the string
It's not to hang ourselves by, it's to see
Beyond ourselves.

NOTES

"Cenote" is one of the last poems I wrote during my senior year of college. It ruminates on the feeling of anxiousness I sometimes hold when I write. It feels like a strangling leash on my own imagination. Writing this poem helped me express that anxiety.

"Koi" is about the first time I went to the *Peace Awareness Labyrinth & Gardens Center* in Los Angeles. They have a tranquil koi pond where I sat and meditated. Just watching them swim, I lost sense of where I was and it turned out that I had been sitting there for quite some time. I dreamed of stories.

"Walking to Hummingbirds" is a significant poem to me in this collection because these two moments actually happened. I saw Alive when I felt very happy and content. I saw Dead at a time when I felt very alone. Seeing a hummingbird fleet by always fills me with joy. The hummingbird is my power animal, and so to see one dead truly struck me in a very painful way.

"Strange Animals" pokes at the notion of being human vs. being humane. You may think *some* people are strange, or might not like the phrasing at all. But, people *are* mammals. It is my belief that no one is better, or more deserving of life, than anything else living in the world. Ideas of separation and superiority that some people and systems foster, have complicated this notion. We need to break this pattern. In order to change this, we have to recognize our judgements, how we think, and what we tolerate.

"Pyrophytic," speaks to the idea that some plants, called pryophytes, *need* fire to release their seeds and germinate. This concept has always fascinated me! Adaptation is a glorious cosmic mother! When we see so many blazing fires in our chaparrals and other places, it's often due to the lack of controlled burns over the years and a host of other environmental issues.

In "Wake Up," I piece together an amalgamation of notes I kept around my thoughts on the murders of Breonna Taylor, Ahmaud Arbery, George Floyd and many other Black people killed during our months in quarantine during 2020. This poem is for every Black body laid to rest too soon, and it's for the protestors bravely disrupting the status quo to create a better world for all of us.

ACKNOWLEDGMENTS

Thank you for the ever constant encouragements, Mom. You never doubted my words, even when I did. Thank you to my dad and brothers for their love and support.

A deep thank you to the writing mentorship program, WriteGirl, for encouraging young girls like me to write. As a proud alumna, I am grateful for having the opportunity to share my first works in their anthologies and to continuously receive their support!

I'm grateful to Pitzer College and the experiences I had while attending the liberal arts school. Many of these poems were inspired by my period of life wandering the campus as well as studying abroad through Pitzer's study abroad program in Costa Rica. To my professors and advisors at Pitzer College, Laura Harris and Brent Armendinger, thank you both tremendously for guiding me in my writing and academic journey. The encouragement and advice I received from you both during my four years has had an incredible impact in my life and in my growing writing career.

Muchas gracias, mi mama tica, Blanca Montero! Thank you for opening your home to me during my study abroad in Costa Rica. I'll always appreciate your efforts to help me identify native plants. Thank you so much for treating me like family.

Much appreciation to Nia McAllister, poet and founder of the Museum of the African Diaspora's open mic night series, MoAD Lit. Thank you for inviting me to share my poems!

Thank you, Changing Womxn Collective for sharing my poem, "Afrofuture" in the second issue of your digital literary journal, *Black & Blooming.*

I want to thank my Soka Gakkai International Buddhist community for encouraging me to be determined and win over life's obstacles. I'm deeply thankful to the SGI members who helped my family weather through a very challenging time in our lives.

ABOUT THE AUTHOR

Kai Adia is a Los Angeles-based writer of short stories, poetry, and prose. She focuses on science fiction and fantasy, as well as realistic fiction and the surreal. She often incorporates themes of nature and environmental concerns into her writing. In 2018, Kai graduated from Pitzer College with a Bachelor of Arts degree in Environmental Analysis and English & World Literature. In 2017, she was awarded the Bea Matas Hollfelder '87 Award by the English Department at Pitzer College for exceptional work in creative writing and literature. As an active community member, Kai has always valued and appreciated artisans and storytellers from diverse cultural backgrounds and experiences. She is constantly inspired to reflect her beautiful world in her work. Currently, Kai is a publicist for a boutique, women-owned PR agency as well as a freelance writer and editor working to help other creators produce and publish their books.

www.ingramcontent.com/pod-product-compliance
Lightning Source LLC
LaVergne TN
LVHW020940090426
835512LV00020B/3438

9 781736 003800